Lee sees a clean sheet.
The sheet seems to fly.

1

The sheet is just what Lee needs.
She takes two seats to the sheet.

Lee pulls the sheet over the seats.
The sheet will make a pretty tent!

Lee will eat a treat in the tent.
"I will keep my tent clean," she says.

Lee peeks from the sheet.
"What a neat place for me," says Lee.

Teeny sees Lee in the tent.
Teeny sees a treat, too.

EEK! Teeny tugs the sheet.
The sheet falls on Lee.

Lee says, "Now, I know what I can be.
I will keep the sheet on me.
I can be a queen!"